INSTANT
VOICE TRAINING

The INSTANT-Series *Presents*

INSTANT

VOICE TRAINING

How to Train Your Voice Instantly!

2nd Edition

Instant Series Publication

ISBN 978-1-530-44452-6

Printed in the United States of America

Second Edition

FIRST STEP:

Before proceeding, visit http://www.instantseries.com, and join the **INSTANT Newsletter** now.

You will want to! :)

CONTENTS

<u>Chapter 1</u>

The Voice of Power

'Say What? I Didn't Hear You!'

You may be wondering, "Why would I want to *train my voice?*"

- Well, have you ever been **talking** with a group of people and noticed that some of them are simply <u>not listening</u> to *what YOU have to say*? Do you have to **repeat** yourself to be heard?

Do you want to **sound more powerful** and **command attention**?

Of course you do!

With a little help and some practice, you can improve just about any area of your life; voice training is no exception.

Many folks assume that if they have a **weak voice,** that's just the voice they were born with, and there's *nothing* they can do about it. *Wrong!* There is good news.

You can **retrain your voice**!

Voice training is a well-kept secret; but in fact, many people have learned to adjust their voices, and **you can too**! Actually, voice training is quite **common**: most singers, as well as many professional speakers and politicians, undergo extensive training.

If you want a little inspiration, just (re)watch *My Fair Lady*: "In Hartford, Hereford, and Hampshire, hurricanes hardly ever happen."

The Goodies Of A Good Voice

But you're not a singer, you say? Or a public speaker? Training your voice can set you up for life, *no matter* your career:

- **You become more confident.** By improving your voice, you will also bolster your *self-confidence* and sense of *self-empowerment.* A confident person speaks a little stronger, stands a little taller, and looks a little bolder. A confident person exudes empowerment, and people react well to confidence. Simply *knowing* that your voice is powerful and that you can make yourself heard will give you the confidence to stride into any room with *purpose,* ready to get things done.

- **You become more influential.** The more control you have over your "vocals" the more impact you'll have on people. Just take a listen to the influential ideological leaders of the past 100 years (whether you agree with them or not), such as Joseph Stalin or Fidel Castro; their voices **reflected power**. When you sound confident, others will be confident in *your* abilities.

- **You become more memorable.** A great voice allows anybody to be taken seriously and makes others listen. Nobody wants to listen to a person who speaks with a grating voice; not only is it irritating, but it also makes people uncomfortable. You might be remembered as having an annoying voice, but no one will remember what you said. Celebrities like George Clooney, Morgan Freeman, and Liam Neeson are able to sustain so much attention *off-screen* partly because they have strong voices that linger in the minds of listeners, leaving an unforgettable **impression**. Such a voice makes people pay attention.

- **You become more attractive.** No, training your voice doesn't change your appearance, but it does change how people <u>react</u> to you. Think of Clarke Gable (**Rhett Butler** in *Gone with the Wind,* if you need a reference). Although his voice wasn't particularly deep or loud, it was commanding, charismatic, and made everyone want to listen. It certainly made women swoon over him and men want to be like him!

<u>Goal</u>: It's All Personal

Think about what **you** want *your voice* to sound like, and write it all down.

- Do you wish to have more control of your voice?

- Do you want to overcome a condition that prevents you from speaking with a clear voice?

- Do you hope to lower your voice so that you sound more confident?

Write everything down. This will guide and motivate you as you progress through your voice training.

Chapter 2

Determine Your Voice Type

The Different Types Of Voices

There are many voices out there, but which one is you?

Before we launch into **vocal techniques**, it's important to think about what kind of voice *you have* and what kind *you want to have*.

But how do we distinguish vocal features?

Here are <u>four main vocal types</u> that will help us talk about different aspects a voice:

Nasal Voice

A **nasal voice**, as its name suggests, sounds as if the speaker is *holding their nose* or *has a cold*. It can occur naturally and permanently in some people.

Generally, people with a nasal voice sound moody and their speech is barely articulated.

Every sound is projected from the nose, so it sounds like the nose is "swallowing" many syllables, and it can be difficult to understand.

> Example*: Instead of "Huh, I don't know… I think I'll pass this time, thank you!" you might hear, "HaaH, I oknow… I zink I'll paass dis dime, zanku!"

*Note: We are just recreating sounds and not implying that people with nasal projections don't know how to talk.

This is technically known as **hyponasality**. There are also conditions, such as a **cleft palate**, that allow too much air to flow through the nose and result in hypernasality.

Mouth Voice

The **mouth voice** (also known as head voice) is not very powerful because it *doesn't have much force* behind it.

People with mouth voices often sound strained, overworked, and uninteresting. Such a voice can sound *annoying* because it is over-articulated.

The vowels also sound too loud, which is irritating to the ears and can even sound aggressive.

Example*: Instead of hearing "I've got no idea as to where he went to, I wasn't there with him" you may hear "I'VE GOT NO IDEA AS TO WHERE HE WEEENT TOOW, I WAAASN'T THERE WWWITH HIIIM."

*Note:** The uppercase letters do not mean that the person is yelling, but that the tone is often *aggressive*, with certain sounds *overstressed* (as if they were amplified through the mouth).

Chest Voice

Chest voice is normally a term used for vocal music to distinguish a lower, throatier sound from the lighter, floaty head voice.

A person speaking with a chest voice might sound *out of breath* because too much stress is put on the heart and lungs.

Chest voices can come across as *overly forceful* and can cause the listener to feel that the speaker is trying to impose his or her views, even if that's not the case.

Example: For "Take the left and go forward," you may hear "TAKETHELEFTANDGO FORWARD!"

Everyone yells in their chest voice, so people who use their chest voice all the time can often sound angry, even if they aren't shouting. As with yelling, the voice is often pitched high and is not well-articulated.

Diaphragm Voice

And finally, the **diaphragm voice** involves projecting from the diaphragm and is considered to be the *most natural-sounding voice* (for both men and women).

The air and sounds are projected from your diaphragm through the length of your torso without any obstructions (you are not cutting it short at the nose, mouth, or throat), so your words emerge *undistorted* and *clear*.

The neck and mouth are perfectly aligned and used to shape the sound, producing *careful articulation*.

<u>Example</u>: "I have a huge passion for music" will be heard clearly, with extra emphasis on the consonants (**bolded+underlined**), especially those that start or end a word: "I <u>**h**</u>ave a <u>**h**</u>uge <u>**p**</u>assio<u>**n**</u> <u>**f**</u>or <u>**m**</u>usi<u>**c**</u>."

<u>Self-Assessment</u>: What Voice Do You Have?

Now, let's see if you can recognize *which* one of these voices resembles **yours**. You might even have elements of *several*.

To help you recognize your voice type, try **recording** your voice (using an audio recorder, your phone, or a recording application on your computer).

Read the <u>following sentence</u>, and then listen carefully to the recording.

"I don't believe in angels, but he was very present in my life."

- Can you hear whether you project more from the nose, chest, mouth, or diaphragm? Think about the different sounds in the sentence, which stick out when you say them, and why they do so.

Chapter 3

Learn Proper Breathing

The Breath-And-Voice Correlation

Why does it matter *how we breathe*? Because breathing is for more than circulating oxygen through our bodies; it prepares us to speak. But because we constantly breathe without thinking about it, and no one teaches us what good breathing entails, it's easy to develop bad habits. Such bad habits can affect your voice.

- For example, bad breathing can interfere with the natural rhythm of speech or cause you to sound timid and unsure. Bad habits can even damage your vocal cords, especially if you overuse your voice, and can worsen with time.

Poor breathing technique and excessive tension in the neck and laryngeal muscles during a speech can both lead to vocal fatigue, increased vocal effort, and hoarseness conditions, such as <u>vocal cord paralysis</u> and <u>paresis</u>.

Fortunately, the use of **vocal techniques** can not only help you overcome these effects, but also help you learn new habits to improve your voice.

Professional voice coaches encourage the use of **breathing exercises** to enhance the quality of your voice. Simply by taking full, deep, relaxed breaths you can enhance the depth and vibrancy of your voice.

Inhaling And Exhaling Stomach Movements

Now...*how can you breathe* and *use your voice* at the same time?

The way you do this is through your **stomach movements**—*expanding your stomach outward* to pull air in when you <u>inhale</u> and *contracting your stomach inward* to push air out when you <u>exhale</u>.

> ***DO NOT MISTAKE** this for inhaling and exhaling with <u>your mouth</u> *simultaneously* as you are moving it to produce speech. Instead, the breathing is all in the movements of <u>your stomach</u> that does the inhaling and exhaling of air while your mouth does the articulating—in other words, non-verbal breathing *via* the movement of your stomach and verbal speaking *via* the movement of your mouth.

So, when **breathing in**, you are simply *inflating* your stomach to draw air in, and when **breathing out**, you are *deflating* your stomach back down to allow air out.

Although our <u>main focus</u> is on your **speaking voice**, singers use their stomach area all the time for breathing while their mouth is singing (which we will get into in the upcoming chapter). Otherwise, how else could they sing an entire song in one go without running out of breath?

When you are talking normally in everyday conversation, the process of taking a breath while speaking will be much subtler.

Breathing Exercise 1: Puff Some Air

So, let's get to work. For this exercise, you will need a place to lie down. Remember that posture is everything, so keep your spine straight.

STEP 1: *Lie down* on your back and begin by breathing in and out. *Inhale* and fill your lungs with air; it should feel like your abdomen (tummy) is full, too, although of course the air is in your lungs, which expand as your diaphragm pulls down. *Exhale* by releasing the air gradually and your torso will deflate. *Start slowly.* As you inhale, count to ten (as if you were counting down seconds for the New Year, not as if you were playing hide and seek and want to start as soon as possible). *Do the same* while you exhale. Don't fill up so fast that you have to hold your breath or so slow that you don't end up with a full breath. *Breathe in and out* steadily as you count, reaching your fullest and emptiest points when you get to <u>ten</u>. Complete <u>three</u> breathing cycles (inhale and exhale).

<u>STEP 2</u>: Now *speed up* your breathing a little bit: count to <u>4</u> when you *inhale* and then <u>4</u> again when you *exhale*. But don't cut yourself short; make sure you breathe quickly enough to fill all the way up by <u>4</u> and empty all the way out by <u>4</u>. You don't want to try running on an empty tank! Complete <u>three</u> breathing cycles. (You have consciously altered your breathing rhythm!) Your breathing rhythm is simply how fast you're breathing and can be represented by what <u>number</u> you count to as you breathe in and out.

STEP 3: As you continue breathing with a rhythm of 4, start **humming** smoothly (make sure not to put pressure on your vocal cords; it should feel easy and comfortable). Stop *before* starting a new breathing cycle and count to 5. Complete three breathing cycles. If you feel an itchy sensation in your throat, don't worry, this is normal. It's actually a sign that your cords are *warming up*; they're just not used to being stimulated this way.

STEP 4: Follow the same breathing pattern, but pronounce the phrase "I want to give" with one word per *inhale* or *exhale*. In other words, the first word, "I," should last the whole inhaling phase (4 seconds), followed by the second word, "want," when you exhale (4 seconds), and so on. Since it's hard to count and speak at the same time, try *tapping your fingers* to maintain your breathing rhythm. Using the four fingers *other* than your thumb, you can tap **one finger** per number (pointer (1), middle (2), ring (3), pinky (4)) as you inhale and exhale. Repeat this step five times.

Make sure that you maintain a straight body posture during the whole process.

Practice this exercise as much as you can. Once you get the hang of it, you can do it **standing up**, too. Whether you choose to *sit down* or *stand up*, remember to keep breathing from your tummy and to keep the same breathing technique and rhythm (count to 4 during each inhale and exhale).

<u>Breathing Exercise 2</u>: Strengthen Diaphragm

This time put a **medium-sized book** on your belly to serve as a weight to strengthen your diaphragm and abdominal muscles. This will help you to sustain a stable breathing rhythm as you speak, because the *pressure* it puts on your abdomen forces you to take a deeper breath and then helps "push" your voice out.

- You can think of this breathing technique as an air pump. First you need to pull the handle out, and then when you push the handle of the pump, air comes out due to the pressure you applied. Here, your diaphragm pulls down, filling your lungs, and then pressure needs to come from your abdomen to release the air gradually.

So now do the <u>same exercise</u> from before, but with the book. Lie down on your back, and put that book on your tummy (not dictionary large, but not tiny paperback either).

<u>STEP 1</u>: Begin by breathing in and out. Inhale, pushing against the book and filling your lungs with air. Then exhale by releasing the air gradually and allowing the book to push down on your abdomen. Count slowly to <u>10</u> for each *inhale* and *exhale* to establish a slow breathing pattern. Complete <u>three</u> breathing cycles.

<u>STEP 2</u>: Speed up your breathing pattern by counting to <u>4</u> when you *inhale* and then <u>4</u> again when you *exhale*. Complete <u>three</u> breathing cycles.

STEP 3: As you continue breathing with a rhythm of 4, start **humming** smoothly (again, don't put too much pressure on your vocal cords). Stop for 5 seconds before you start a new breathing cycle. Complete three cycles.

STEP 4: Follow the same breathing pattern, but pronounce the phrase "I want to give" with one word per *inhale* or *exhale*, as before. Remember to *tap your fingers* to help you count your breathing rhythm. Repeat this step at least 5 times.

Result: Altered Breathing Rhythm

Consider the following questions:

- After practicing this technique, do you notice yourself breathing differently during the day? What are the differences?

- How consistent is your breathing now? When is it the best? When is it the worst?

- How do you think your breathing help with the quality of your voice? What differences do you notice? How fast did you notice them?

Other Vocal Factors

Please bear in mind that proper breathing is not the only component for yielding a better voice. There are <u>other criteria</u> to consider such as habitual lifestyle, healthy diet, and *uncontrollable* physical aspects like facial structure.

- In some cases, even seeing an orthodontist can improve your voice, *e.g.*, correcting an overbite or jaw misalignment that is preventing you from having full mouth control and hampering the ease with which you speak.

Essentially there are a lot of factors involved in how one's voice sounds. Breathing, *however*, just happens to be the easiest factor that you can control and *why* it is given the most attention here.

Proper breathing while speaking is a habit, so don't fret if learning to breathe properly doesn't immediately make a huge difference in your current voice yet. It will all be reviewed later in the <u>cumulative chapter</u> after you have grasped further general knowledge about voice training.

- We will get more into food, nutrition, best practices, lifestyle choices, as well as the one exercise that you'll ever need (**"mouth pull-ups"**) which will have a far *greater impact* on your voice later.

Thus, this is only the *tip of the iceberg*.

Chapter 4

Work on Vocal Projection

Singing Meets Speaking

Regardless of musical tastes, almost everyone has been fascinated with great vocalists such as Adele, Whitney Houston, and Mariah Carey, or operatic artists such as Luciano Pavarotti and Renée Fleming.

You may have asked yourself how they have such powerful voices. People will tell you that most of these performers "*sing from their diaphragm*," the dome-shaped muscular partition separating the chest from the abdomen.

Singers who breathe and project from their diaphragm sound as if their voices come all the way from their bellies, while many other people sound as if their voices come from the chest or throat.

Think about your favorite singers again, just for a moment. If you watch them sing, you'll notice that their shoulders don't move, but their stomachs do. This is because they're breathing from their diaphragm and not their chest. You may also notice that they flex their knees or rise up on their toes. This isn't just showmanship; it actually makes it *easier* for them to sing.

Whether you're a singer or not, projecting from the diaphragm to improve your **talking voice** is the way to go. It's a bit like injecting some *singing* into your *speaking*, and the results can be phenomenal!

Speaking doesn't require as much conscious work as singing does, but if you want to improve the quality of your speaking voice, using singing techniques can help you, just as they help professional singers!

Chest Voice vs. Diaphragm Voice

You've already practiced breathing, so now let's move on to *your voice* itself.

Try to compare your **chest voice** to your **diaphragm voice** by *projecting your voice* from <u>each place</u>. Don't know how to do that? Don't worry, just follow these directions.

> 1.) First, breathe in shallowly, just filling your lungs at the top. Then, try to project your voice from your **chest**. Make a series of *humming sounds* for <u>one minute</u>.

Do you feel how much effort it takes and how much *strain* it puts on your lungs? Also, after a short time, your voice starts to change and fade, right? If you have trouble figuring out how to project from your chest, don't worry.

After all, it's *not* the way you should be breathing; you *should* be breathing from the diaphragm.

2.) So now, do the same thing as before. Breathe deeply, but this time project your voice from your **diaphragm** with a series of <u>20</u> short *humming sounds* (for a total duration of <u>one minute</u>). This technique involves contracting the muscles in your tummy so it would help to put your hands on your belly to feel and control those muscles as you practice.

You'll probably find that your voice has more consistency and are more comfortable throughout the process. That's because you are breathing and projecting properly, pushing the sounds from your diaphragm through your chest, mouth, and nose, rather than directly from any one of those locations.

But how do you perfect this technique?

First, it will take a few sessions to really understand what projecting from the diaphragm involves. And then you need to develop the habit of breathing and projecting from there so that you can do it unconsciously.

<u>Projection Exercise 1</u>: Project From The Diaphragm

So, how do you train yourself to project effectively? Here's another exercise with more detailed instructions.

<u>STEP 1</u>: In a *standing position*, relax yourself. *Inhale* (one), and *exhale* (two) both through the mouth. Repeat this cycle <u>once</u> more.

<u>STEP 2</u>: Breathe in, *place your tongue* on the ridge of your mouth, behind your upper teeth, push from your stomach, let the pressure fill your torso, and pronounce "do." (It should feel as if the pressure you were putting on your abdominals was pushing the "do" sound out of your mouth, despite your best efforts.) When you

pronounce the sound it shouldn't be forced. The note should sort of linger for a moment: "doooo!"

STEP 3: Pronounce "do" 15 times, each time pushing the air from below your abdominals and using your hand to imitate the air rushing towards your mouth. *Put your hands* in front of your chest and *move them* upwards (as if you were asking someone to stand up).

STEP 4: Pronounce the following sentence: "Do we have to be rea-dy to-mo-rrow?" Remember to breathe in deeply with your diaphragm and then push your abdominals (contracting your tummy each time you pronounce a syllable). As you pronounce each syllable, *lift your body up* by standing on the tip of your toes (with your hands still in front of your chest making the *same movement* as before). This will help you to control your abdominal muscles. Repeat this step 8 times, taking a step forward with each syllable as you rise to your toes. Walk around the room this way; it will help the process feel more routine and natural.

Great job, you've begun to use your diaphragm to project your voice! But apart from an exercise, you need do this regularly while speaking. Every time you speak, adopt the right position and push your voice from your tummy.

At first, you'll have to do this purposefully, but eventually it will become automatic. So before you speak, remember to breathe deeply and contract your abdominals, imagining that you are actually thrusting your voice up through your chest so that it can find an exit through your mouth.

<u>Projection Exercise 2</u>: More Projecting

Now let's practice with the following exercise:

<u>STEP 1</u>: Use your hands to put pressure on your tummy. As you press, gradually contract your muscles. As your muscles contract, *lift your rib cage* and then release the air.

STEP 2: Make a "do" sound while you push the air through the air column and release it from your mouth. You will notice that the "do" comes out clearly, and as you release it, you exhale automatically (releasing your abdominal muscles at the same time). Repeat this process 10 times. Don't forget to use your abdominal muscles and hands to keep putting pressure on your abdomen.

STEP 3: Using the same technique, speak the following sentence, one syllable at a time: "Do-I-have-to-be-tall?"

STEP 4: Repeat five times, but putting *extra stress* on each syllable: "dooo-iiiiii-hhhaaaavvvvvve-tooo-beeee-taaaallll?"

STEP 5: Finally, pronounce the sentence at normal speed, but still using the pressure from your belly: "Do I have to be tall?" Repeat 5 times.

Result: Adjusted Projection

Consider the following questions:

- Do you hear any difference with your voice now? What's different from the way you normally speak?

- How does it feel to have your speaking voice coming out of your belly? How is this different from the way it usually feels?

<u>Chapter 5</u>

Sustain Sound Control

Overused Sustainability

All of this voice training is useful, but you also need to be able to maintain it when speaking.

Even if you sound like Sean Connery at one moment, if the next you're as raspy as Casey Affleck and trailing off at the end of sentences, like a coach who's spent all day screaming at his players, your audience will wonder whether your body has been hijacked by extraterrestrial life forms.

The point is, you don't want to sound great only when you focus all of your attention on the mechanics of speaking, only to lose that sound—and your confidence—the moment you are distracted. This is especially true if you have an important upcoming event that requires the prolonged use of your magnificent voice. You don't want to not have it when you need it.

Consistent sustainability is the goal, not just temporary tricks.

<u>Control Exercise 1</u>: Read Out Loud

Before you try something nerve-racking like speaking publically, practice by **reading out loud**. This allows you to practice both the *speaking* itself, and *listening* for adjustments.

1.) Begin by breathing in and out quickly and trying to maintain a stable tone. **Don't be dramatic**: do not scream, groan, or yell. Use a *moderate* and *audible tone*, just as you would if you were reading a manual for the first time and trying to figure out what to do.

As an example, try reading the following familiar <u>story</u> from the Brothers Grimm:

> "Once upon a time there was a sweet little girl. Everyone who saw her liked her, but most of all her grandmother, who did not know what to give the child next. Once she gave her a little cap made of red velvet. Because it suited her so well, and she wanted to wear it all the time, she came to be known as Little Red Cap. One day her mother said to her, 'Come Little Red Cap. Here is a piece of cake and a bottle of wine. Take them to your grandmother.'"

Note: Try to *maintain the same pitch and tone* as you read. It can be tempting to read quickly until you get to the exciting part, but don't rush; use a *natural calm rhythm*. If your throat becomes irritated as you progress through your reading, you probably underuse your speaking voice, and it's getting tired. Carry on for a little while, but don't push it. With time you will feel less of this irritation as your vocal cords become accustomed to it.

2.) Read the <u>above text again</u>, this time elevating the tone of your voice slightly; do not scream, groan, or yell, just use a *slightly louder* (and possibly higher) tone than before, as if you were reading the text to a small group of people.

If you're not used to reading aloud you *may experience some discomfort*, such as a scratchy throat, coughing, or even a buildup of mucus. Don't worry. This is normal; your voice just isn't used to working so hard!

Remember that to improve your vocal abilities you have to work on your vocal cords, but just like any other muscle, you don't want to overstrain it by working it too hard all at once. You can start with *shorter practice sessions*, lengthening them gradually as your vocal strength increases.

3.) Next, read the <u>same passage</u> one more time at a *lower volume*, as if you were reading to yourself. But still breathe and project from your diaphragm. Just because it's quieter doesn't mean you don't have to project!

After this first session, you should feel more comfortable projecting at different volumes. As you continue to practice, consider what tone is best for each situation. How many people are you talking to? How big is the room?

<u>Control Exercise 2</u>: Vocal Sit-Ups

Here's one last exercise to strengthen all the muscles involved in speaking, including your vocal cords, your diaphragm, and your abdominal muscles.

Start by reading the following line *loudly*, as to a group of <u>15 people</u>:

<u>Line 1</u>: "I would rather climb a mountain than go through all of this!"

<u>Line 2</u>: Then, at the same volume, stretch out each word and read the line like this: "Iiiiiii- wouuuuuld-raaather-cliiiiimb-aaaaa-mountaiiinnnnn-thaaaan-goooooo-throuuuuuugh-aaaall-ooooof-thiiiiiiisssssss!"

And now come the **vocal sit-ups**: you will alternate between your normal, moderate volume (not too high, not too low) and a louder, but still speaking, volume.

Read the **bolded+underlined words** in a louder voice.

<u>Line 1</u>: "I **<u>would</u>** rather **<u>climb</u>** a **<u>Mountain</u>** than **<u>go</u>** through **<u>all</u>** of **<u>this</u>**!" (Repeat this line <u>3 times</u>.)

Then read <u>line 2</u>, dragging out each word, but again alternating your tone:

<u>Line 2</u>: "**<u>iiiiii</u>**-wouuuuuld-**<u>Raaather</u>**-Cliiiiimb-**<u>aaaaa</u>**-Mountaiiinnnnn-**<u>Thaaaan</u>**-goiiiiiiiing-**<u>Throuuuuuugh</u>**-aaaall-**<u>ooooof</u>**-Thiiiiiiisssssss!" (Repeat this line <u>3 times</u>.)

By doing this, you are training your vocal cords to *adjust* to your <u>desired volume</u>. This gives you more **control** over your vocal cords and allows you to speak clearly for longer periods of time.

Of course, you can change things up by using different sentences. You can try "The baby cried all night, preventing the parents from finishing their work," or any other sentence that has a good variety of sounds.

If you practice exercising your voice regularly, you will feel your vocal cords start to adapt, and ultimately you'll develop a voice that sounds stronger, more confident, and more mature.

Chapter 6

Level Up to Golden Voice

The Vocal-Crash Boot Camp

Now that you're exposed to voice training and know how to use your voice properly, here are additional exercises to continue strengthening your voice.

Note: You can refer to this <u>section</u> only whenever you need a quick, handy-dandy guide to get your voice in top-performing shape. It's basically a cumulative review of everything we've gone over and more.

Warm-Up: The Mouth Pull-Ups

Before you do anything, let's warm up and flex your mouth and jaw muscles.

First, stretch your mouth by doing some opening and closing it all the way, then push your lower jaw *in-and-out*, follow by *side-to-side*. This will loosen up any stiffness.

Now close your mouth, push your lips together tightly, and say "Ummm-Hmmm" with as much control and rising inflection as possible (keeping your mouth closed and feeling the tingling sensation).

STEP 1: First, do this once standing up with arms at your sides, saying "Ummm-Hmmm."

STEP 2: Next, raise both arms in the air, as high as you can reach, and say "Ummm-Hmmm."

STEP 3: Then, bend forward as far as you can comfortably, dangle your arms in front of you, and say "Ummm-Hmmm."

STEP 4: Finally, return to your upright standing position, with both arms at your sides, for a final "Ummm-Hmmm."

You should notice a difference in your voice. It should be clearer and more controlled now that you've warmed things up and moved around a bit.

Think of this voice exercise as if you were in the gym doing pull-ups with weights shackled to your feet. After adding the burden of heavier weights (mouth closed, different positions), once you remove that burden (upright, mouth opened again), your body finds it easier to perform.

Ideally, do this when you get up in the morning to *pull your voice forward* again, after a night of lying down *pushing your voice* to the back.

Voice Exercise 1: The Fresh Breath

A. Preparation

(This part should sound familiar!)

STEP 1: Begin by *slowly breathing* in and out. Inhale with your diaphragm and fill your lungs with air, then exhale by releasing the air slowly and pushing out from your abdomen. Establish a steady rhythm by counting to 10 for each *inhale* and *exhale*. Complete three breathing cycles.

STEP 2: *Speed up* the breathing pattern by counting to 4 each time you *inhale* or *exhale*. Complete three breathing cycles.

STEP 3: As you continue breathing with a rhythm of 4, start **humming** smoothly (remember, don't put too much pressure on your vocal cords). Stop for 5 seconds before you start a new breathing cycle. Complete three breathing cycles.

STEP 4: Follow the same breathing pattern, but pronounce the phrase "I want to give" with one word per *inhale* or *exhale*. In other words, the first word, "I," should last the whole inhaling phase (4 seconds), followed by the second word, "want," when you exhale (4 seconds), and so on. Since it's hard to count and speak at the same time, try tapping your fingers to maintain your breathing rhythm. Using the four fingers *other* than your thumb, you can tap **one finger** per number (pointer (1), middle (2), ring (3), pinky (4)) as you inhale and exhale. Repeat this step at least five times.

B. Performance
(Put your training to the test!)

Use the same breathing technique to read the following sentences. Try to sustain a good breathing rhythm by reading the lines at a moderate pace (not too fast, not to slow).

"I used to eat five times a day, until school started, and I realized that almost everybody else was a size zero."

"His car was speeding; that's why the cops stopped him, last night."

"Being 22 wasn't a problem for Anna as she constantly tried to be someone she wasn't."

- Did you run out of breath easily, while you were reading? When did you run out of breath? Why?

<u>Voice Exercise 2</u>: The Diaphragm Flex

Use diaphragm projection to contract your abdominals and push the sound through your body and out of your mouth.

Practice it by reading the <u>following text</u>:

> "Chromos was the name of the planet. I
> ain't lying. The aliens abducted me and took
> me there. It's a green planet, covered by a lot
> of vegetation. The animals are weird and too
> big. It was a strange experience, almost like
> living on the planet of apes or something."

Try to strengthen your diaphragm and abdominal muscles by pronouncing *each syllable* <u>three times</u> ("chro-chro-chro, mos-mos-mos, was-was-was..."). Then, still projecting from your diaphragm, read the text normally (full words) <u>three times</u>.

- How would you describe the quality of your voice after using this technique a few times? Has it changed?

<u>Voice Exercise 3</u>: The Sound Of Your Voice

Alternate vocal strength, as before, by reading aloud the <u>following line</u>:

"I **<u>would</u>** like **<u>to</u>** eat **<u>some</u>** of **<u>the</u>** prunes **<u>that</u>** are **<u>on</u>** the **<u>counter</u>**!"

Remember to read the **bolded+underlined words** at a *higher volume*. Repeat the process <u>five times</u>. Don't stop the exercise, even if you feel an itchy sensation in your throat.

- Can you hear or feel an improvement? How would you rate your voice on a scale of <u>0</u> to <u>10</u>, after doing this exercise? How has it changed?

<u>Self-Assessment</u>: The Before And After

Now that you've gone through all of the voice exercises, it's time to record **your voice** again.

Take a deep breath and *record yourself* saying:

> "I will never have the chance to hold this position again, since Mavis is back for good."

- Can you tell if your tone or pitch has improved? How has your voice changed?

- Do you still feel any discomfort (if you felt any during your very first exercises)?

- Are you now projecting from your diaphragm? Why do you think you are or aren't? Are you consistent?

Chapter 7

Maintain the Voice for Life

Throat Nourishments

Voice exercises may help us develop our vocal capacities, but that means nothing if we don't also take care of our throat.

As with anything else related to your body, if you want to maintain a clear and healthy voice, you have to watch what you eat. Some things soothe your throat, while others can irritate it or make it difficult to articulate properly.

What to Avoid:

- Caffeine-based Drinks and Alcoholic Beverages

Especially coffee, caffeinated soda, and strong alcohol. Caffeine and alcohol are both natural diuretics (they cause an excessive passing of urine), so they can cause your throat muscles to become *dehydrated*, leading to muscle constriction. This can make it more difficult for you to produce a pleasant, smooth sound. Over a long period of time, it can even lead to damaged vocal cords, causing hoarseness, strain, or even the loss of your voice (or vocal ability). When you do drink caffeine or alcohol, be sure to stay well-hydrated by **drinking water** too.

- Dairy and Dairy Products

Dairy products are perhaps the most important things to *avoid* <u>right before</u> a **speech** or **performance**. Milk and milk products—including yogurt, cheese, ice cream, and butter—increase **phlegm production** in your throat. The extra mucous makes it difficult to speak clearly and causes you to clear your throat constantly. They're not actually bad for you, so you don't have to cut them from your diet, but you should avoid eating or drinking dairy products <u>just</u> <u>before</u> an interview, speech, singing performance, etc.

<u>What to Indulge</u>:

- Hydrating Foods
Staying well-hydrated is important if you want to have a healthy voice. Drink enough fluids during the day, especially **water**. Also eat fruits and vegetables that are naturally high in water, such as apples, grapes, peaches, raw tomatoes, celery, or cucumber.

- Foods High in Vitamin A
Vitamin A helps keep your soft tissue, skin, and mucous membranes healthy. And luckily, it's found in a large variety of foods. Vitamin A is found in high quantities in eggs and meat. If you don't eat meat, try yellow and orange fruits and vegetables such as orange sweet peppers, carrots, apricots, and cantaloupe, as well as dark, leafy greens such as kale and spinach.

- Honey and Mint

Honey is great for soothing a sore throat, especially in some warm herbal tea. You can also substitute honey for sugar, or dribble some on your waffles or pancakes. Minty candies are also a soothing treat to help you clear your throat.

Articulation Best Practices

If you want to speak more clearly, here are a few more tricks:

- **Loosen your jaws** when you speak. Stop trying to speak with your mouth barely open! Open up your mouth and let the sound out. If you're having trouble, pretend to yawn, stretching your mouth all the way open. Then close it part way, but leaving space for the sound to resonate inside your mouth.

- Use your mouth to **shape the sound**. Try to recreate the shape of vowels or sounds with your mouth, so the "a" sound of "grass" should be pronounced with your jaw lowered, while the "o" within "open" should be said with your lips rounded. Use all the muscles supporting your mouth to pronounce your "e," "t," etc. *Don't be lazy!*

- For sounds that need more pressure on your abdomen, such as "e," **close your jaw** a little (but leave space inside). This helps make sure you're not wasting air, and there's nothing more beautiful than showing a little bit of a smile when you speak.

- **Use your tongue** properly. Don't let it flop half way. Push it behind your upper teeth for sounds such as "n" and "l."

By properly articulating, everything you say will be clearer, so you won't strain your throat by talking too loudly just trying to be heard.

Healthy Voice Habits

Here are some simple habits you can take up to help keep your voice in shape and prevent problems in the first place.

1. **Take warm showers.** Especially if you have a nasal voice. A warm shower in the morning clears out your nose, and you'll feel and sound better for hours.

2. **Clear your throat** every morning with a quick gargle. It removes mucous that may have built up overnight. But don't overdo it. A five-second gargle with warm water and a little bit of salt is enough. A longer gargle will only irritate your throat and voice.

3. **Sleep!** This one sounds like a no-brainer, but we all know that getting enough sleep can be difficult. If you have an event coming up and haven't gotten enough sleep, try taking a quick nap. Your voice will thank you later.

4. **Do not smoke,** or if you already do, **quit.** Not only does smoking increase the risk of throat cancer

tremendously, but simply inhaling smoke (even secondhand smoke) can lead to damage to your vocal cords.

5. This may be the hardest of them all, especially if you like parties and concerts: **avoid yelling** or **screaming** and try not to talk in noisy areas where you have to speak loudly to be heard. All of these strain your voice and can cause damage. If your throat feels dry or your voice is getting hoarse, use your voice less, because your vocal cords are tired and irritated.

<u>Chapter 8</u>

You Are the Voice

Voice Commander YOU

Your voice can say a lot about you. It can help you make an astounding impression during that job interview or gain other people's utmost respect.

Unfortunately, we aren't explicitly taught elocution these days, so we have to figure all this out for ourselves.

Singers, especially, rely on their voice more than others, and are the extreme masters at it. Yet thinking about the similarities between singing and speaking, the **solution** is quite simple: *It's all about the breathing. And practice makes perfect.*

So anytime you have a moment to reflect before using your voice, think about your breathing and control your inhaling and exhaling. This will help you control your voice, and command with confidence.

May The Voice Be With You

Dedicate a few minutes of <u>each day</u> to developing your voice because a better voice leads to a better life.

When you speak, start with a deep breath and project from your belly. Judge who your audience is and the size of the environment, and adjust your volume appropriately.

Practice daily by reading aloud to yourself, a friend, or a family member. You can do this.

Your voice is an important part of you. It's your default method of communicating with people. If you don't take care of it, you might end up missing out on crucial opportunity, or you might stay silent when you need to speak up the most. So hone it!

Go ahead and start today; and may your voice guide you.

An INSTANT Thank You!

Thank you for entrusting in the <u>INSTANT Series</u> to help you improve your life.

Our goal is simple, help you achieve instant results as fast as possible in the quickest amount of time. We hope we have done our job, and you have gotten a ton of value.

If you are in any way, shape, or form, dissatisfied, then please we encourage you to get refunded for your purchase because we only want our readers to be happy.

If, *on the other hand*, you've enjoyed it, if you can kindly leave us a review on where you have purchased this book, that would mean a lot.

What is there to do now?

Simple! Head over to http://www.instantseries.com, and sign up for our **newsletter** to stay up-to-date with the latest instant developments *(if you haven't done so already)*.

Be sure to check other books in the INSTANT Series. If there is something you like to be added, be sure to let us know for as always we love your feedback.

Yes, we're on **social medias**. *Don't forget to follow us!*

https://www.facebook.com/InstantSeries

https://twitter.com/InstantSeries

https://plus.google.com/+Instantseries

Thank you, and wish you all the best!
- *The INSTANT Series Team*

Printed in Great Britain
by Amazon

44218979R00046